The
SMALL and MIGHTY
Book of

KNOCK
KNOCK

Jokes

MIX
Paper from
responsible sources
FSC® C020056

Published in 2023 by OH!
An Imprint of Welbeck Non-Fiction Limited,
part of Welbeck Publishing Group.
Offices in: London – 20 Mortimer Street, London W1T 3JW
and Sydney – Level 17, 207 Kent St. Sydney NSW 2000 Australia
www.welbeckpublishing.com

Compilation text © Welbeck Non-Fiction Limited 2023
Design © Welbeck Non-Fiction Limited 2023

ISBN 978-1-80069-543-6

Written and compiled by: Malcolm Croft
Editorial: Matt Thomlinson
Project manager: Russell Porter
Design: Tony Seddon
Production: Freencky Portas

A CIP catalogue for this book is available from the British Library

Printed in China

10 9 8 7 6 5 4 3 2 1

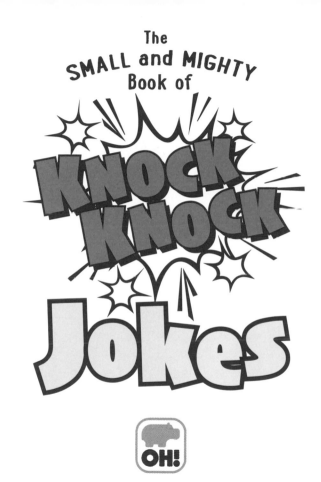

The
SMALL and MIGHTY
Book of

KNOCK
KNOCK

Jokes

OH!

CONTENTS

INTRODUCTION

If it's true (and it's probably not) that England's greatest writer, William Shakespeare, invented the Knock, Knock joke in 1606 – around the time your parents were born – then the type of jokes in this tiny tome have made eyes roll, noses snort and mouths chuckle – as well as a few ears cry – for centuries. Yes, Knock, Knocks are surely a contender for the world's oldest joke, which would make sense given how tired and worn-out most of them feel.

Encouraging giggles and groans in equal measure, with endless punning potential, Knock, Knock jokes are wholesome family fun for kids of all ages. We think of them as stink bombs but without the horrible smell.

This little book is the A-Z of the very best of the very worst Knock, Knock jokes. From Animals to things beginning with Z (we can't think of any right now) the jests inside this gag-fest have been squeezed out from a whole range of hilarious topics, including everyone's favourites – poo, wee and farts.

As you'll soon discover, Knock, Knock jokes come in all shapes and sizes and subjects. Some of the jokes within are more (in)famous than others; some are classics; some are silly; some are new; and some have travelled from around the world just to be here. And, yeah, some of the really funny ones we made up just for you. You're welcome. (Good luck finding them). All of them deserve to be celebrated!

We pinky-promise every one of these jokes has been hand selected by an expert to ensure each one is punnier, and pungent, than the previous page. Put simply: these Knock, Knocks are no knock-offs – they'll blow your socks off! And that's a guarantee (though not a legally binding one).

Remember, don't knock 'em 'til you've tried 'em. Enjoy!

Please don't binge on too many Knock, Knock jokes at once. You might puke. Snack on them lightly throughout the day. And keep this book away from your Dad. Don't encourage him.

KNOCK-OUTS!

World-famous and beloved, these classic Knock, Knock jokes are the best of the best, pure knockouts!

If you're looking for vintage knockers that everyone knows and loves - stop. You've found them.

Only one question remains: Which door will you knock on first?

Knock, Knock

Who's there?

Europe

Europe who?

No, you're a poo!

Knock Knock!

Who's there?

Iron Man

Iron Man who?

You don't know who Iron Man is?

Knock, Knock

Who's there?

Smellmop

Smellmop who?

Ew! No thanks!*

*Make sure you wave your hand in front of
your nose – for extra effect!

Knock, Knock

Who's there?

Nana

Nana who?

Nana your business, that's who!

Knock, Knock

Who's there?

Dishes

Dishes who?

Dishes the police, open up!

Knock, Knock

Who's there?

Disguise

Disguise who?

Disguise the limit!

Knock, Knock

Who's there?

Candice

Candice who?

Candice door open, or am I stuck out here?

Knock, Knock

Who's there?

Says

Says who?

Says me, that's who!

Knock, Knock

Who's there?

Justin

Justin who?

Justin time to smell my fart!*

*Always good to follow up with a really smelly fart!

Knock, Knock

Who's there?

Ice cream

Ice cream who?

Ice cream if you don't open the door!

Knock, Knock

Who's there?

Alex

Alex who?

Alex plain in
a minute.

Knock, Knock

Who's there?

Cereal

Cereal who?

Cereal pleasure to meet you!

Knock, Knock

Who's there?

Olive

Olive who?

Olive next door – hi neighbour!

Knock, Knock

Who's there?

Eggs

Eggs who?

Eggstremely happy to see you!

Knock, Knock

Who's there?

Deja

Deja-who?

Knock, Knock

Knock, Knock

Who's there?

Yacht

Yacht who?

Yacht to know me by now!

Knock, Knock

Who's there?

Radio

Radio who?

Radio not, here I come!

Knock, Knock

Who's there?

Iva

Iva who?

I'VE A SORE HAND FROM ALL THIS DOOR KNOCKING!

KNOCKOUTS!

Knock, Knock

Who's there?

Horsp

Horsp who?

Made you say horse poo!

Knock, Knock

Who's there?

Kent

Kent who?

Kent you tell by my voice?

Knock, Knock

Who's there?

Sarah

Sarah who?

Sarah doorbell I could use?

Knock, Knock

Who's there?

Ferdie

Ferdie who?

Ferdie last time... open the door!

Knock, Knock

Who's there?

YOU

You who?

You-hoo,
anybody home?

Knock, knock!

Who's there?

Cliff Hanger

Cliff Hanger who?*

*Now... just silently walk away!

Knock, Knock

Who's there?

Luke

Luke who?

Luke through the key hole and see!

Knock, Knock

Who's there?

Spell

Spell who?

W H O

Knock, Knock

Who's there?

Mustache

Mustache who?

I mustache you a question, but I'll shave it for later!

Knock, Knock

Who's there?

Cash

Cash who?

No thanks, I prefer macadamias!

Knock, Knock

Who's there?

Lettuce

Lettuce who?

Lettuce in, it's cold out here!

Knock, Knock

Who's there?

Cow says

Cow says who?

No, a cow says moo!*

*But, obviously, moo like a cow. MOOOOO!

Knock, Knock

Who's there?

Tank

Tank who?

You're welcome.

Knock, Knock

Who's there?

Adore

Adore who?

Adore is between you and me. Can you open it?

Knock, Knock

Who's there?

Figs

Figs who?

Figs the doorbell, will ya? I've been knocking for ages!

Knock, Knock

Who's there?

Annie

Annie who?

Annie thing you can do, I can do better!

Knock, Knock

Who's there?

Woo

Woo who?

I'm glad you're excited too, but can you let me in?

Knock, Knock

Who's there?

Two-wit-too

Two-wit too who?

Is there an owl in here?

Knock, Knock

Who's there?

Needle

Needle who?

Needle little help opening the door?

Knock, Knock

Who's there?

Goat

Goat who?

Goat to the door and find out!

Knock, Knock

Who's there?

Toodle

Toodle who?

OK, bye! *

*Don't forget to walk away!

Knock, Knock

Who's there?

Sue

Sue who?

Sue-prize!*

*Shout this really loudly in their face!

Knock Knock

Who's there?

Wendy

Wendy who?

Wendy bell is fixed
I won't have to
knock knock on the
door anymore.

Knock Knock

Who's there?

THE DOORBELL REPAIR MAN.

Knock, Knock

Who's there?

Theodore

Theodore who?

Theodore wasn't open, that's why I knocked!

Knock, Knock

Who's there?

Nobel

Nobel who?

Nobel... that's why I knocked!

Knock, Knock

Who's there?

Anita

Anita who?

Anita wee, open the door!

Knock, Knock

Who's there?

Alec

Alec who?

Alectricity!

*Don't forget to shake your body! BUZZ!

Knock, Knock
Knock, Knock
Knock, Knock
Knock, Knock
Knock, Knock
Knock, Knock

Who's there?

A woodpecker

Knock, Knock

Who's there?

THOR

Thor who?

I THOR YOU KNEW.

CHAPTER
TWO

HARD KNOCK LIFE

It's a hard knock life being a Knock, Knock gag. Everyone thinks of you as one massive joke even though you're just being silly.

To celebrate their awesomeness, we're now serving up the wackiest, wild and weird Knock, Knocks to ever go a-knockin'.

Get ready to go bonkers.

Knock, Knock

Who's there?

Olive

Olive who?

Olive you too!

Knock, Knock

Who's there?

Cockadoodle

Cockadoodle who?

Time
to wake up!

Knock, Knock

Who's there?

Kanga

Kanga who?

Actually, it's pronounced kangaroo.

Knock, Knock

Who's there?

Mikey

Mikey who?

Mikey doesn't work - that's why I'm knocking!

Knock, Knock

Who's there?

Icy

Icy who?

Icy you but I'm not letting you in!

Knock, Knock

Who's there?

A HERD

A herd who?

A HERD THAT FART, DON'T DENY IT!

Knock, Knock

Who's there?

Cargo

Cargo who?

Car go
vroom vroom.

Knock, Knock

Who's there?

A little old lady

A little old lady who?

You're pretty bad at yodelling.

Knock, Knock

Who's there?

Hatch

Hatch who?

Gesundheit!

Knock, Knock

Who's there?

Wooden shoe

Wooden shoe who?

Wooden shoe like to know.

Knock, Knock

Who's there?

Beehive

Beehive who?

Beehive yourself or you can't come in.

Knock, Knock

Who's there?

HOWARD

Howard who?

HOWARD YOU LIKE A BIG SLOPPY KISS?

Knock, Knock

Who's there?

Frank

Frank who?

Frank you for coming!

Knock, Knock

Who's there?

Yaw who?

Howdy there, cowboy!

Knock, Knock

Who's there?

Wire

Wire who?

Wire you always asking me questions?

Knock, Knock

Who's there?

Norma Lee

Norma Lee who?

Norma Lee, I knock and run!

Knock, Knock

Who's there?

Althea

Althea who?

Althea later alligator!

Knock, Knock

Who's there?

Wanda

Wanda who?

Wanda who's knocking on my door.

Knock, Knock

Who's there?

I am

I am who?

You're _____, did you forget your name? *

*Insert their name here!

Knock, Knock

Who's there?

Ho ho

Ho ho who?

That's a terrible Santa impression!

Knock, Knock

Who's there?

Cook

Cook who?

Are you going mad?

Knock, Knock

Who's there?

I did up

I did up who?

You did a poo? Ew!

Knock, Knock

Who's there?

Doris

Doris who?

Doris locked that's why I'm knocking!

Knock, Knock

Who's there?

IMPATIENT COW

Impatient cow...

Mooo!

Knock, Knock

Who's there?

Toucan

Toucan who?

Toucan play this game! Who's there?

Knock, Knock

Who's there?

Hawaii

Hawaii who?

I'm fine, Hawaii you?

Knock, Knock

Who's there?

Beets

Beets who?

Beets me!

Knock, Knock

Who's there?

i.o.

i.o. who?

You owe me. When are you paying me back?

Knock, Knock

Who's there?

Kenya

Kenya who?

Kenya feel the love tonight?*

*Sing this, like from *The Lion King*!

Knock, Knock

Who's there?

HARRY

Harry who?

HARRY UP WILL YA!

Knock, Knock

Who's there?

Avenue

Avenue who?

Avenue got a new doorbell yet?

Knock, Knock

Who's there?

Weevil

Weevil who?

Weevil, weevil rock you!*

*Sing it loud!

Knock, Knock

Who's there?

Viper

Viper who?

Viper nose, you got a big bogey dangling!

Knock, Knock

Who's there?

Scott

Scott who?

Scott nothing to do with you!

Knock, Knock

Who's there?

Dewey

Dewey who?

Dewey have to go to school today?

Knock, Knock

Who's there?

Goliath

Goliath who?

Goliath down, you look-eth sleepy.

Knock, Knock

Who's there?

Amish

Amish who?

Why?
Where am I going?

Knock, Knock

Who's there?

Kiwi

Kiwi who?

Kiwi not do this now.

Knock, Knock

Who's there?

Juno

Juno who?

Juno how to open this door? I want to come in.

Knock, Knock

Who's there?

Teresa

Teresa who?

Teresa green!

CHAPTER
THREE

DON'T KNOCK IT TIL YOU'VE TRIED IT!

The following Knock, Knock jokes may seem terrible at first whiff, proper stinkers. But, we promise if you give them a chance you may just grow to love them.

As your parents always moan about vegetables – don't knock it until you've tried it! Besides, what's the worst that could happen?

Knock, Knock

Who's there?

Butch

Butch who?

Butch your arms around me and give me a hug!

Knock, Knock

Who's there?

REPEAT

Repeat who?

WHO, WHO, WHO, WHO, WHO, WHO, WHO, WHO, WHO.

DON'T KNOCK IT TIL YOU'VE TRIED IT!

Knock, Knock

Who's there?

Noah

Noah who?

Noah? I love her!

Knock, Knock

Who's there?

Lemmy

Lemmy who?

Lemmy in and I'll tell you!

Knock, Knock

Who's there?

Says

Says who?

Says me,
that's who.

Knock, Knock

Who's there?

Imogen

Imogen who?

Imogen life without me!

Knock, Knock

Who's there?

House

House who?

House-who can let you me in?

Knock, Knock

Who's there?

Armageddon

Armageddon who?

Armageddon angry if you don't open this door!

Knock, Knock

Who's there?

Jamaican

Jamaican who?

Jamaican me crazy with all these questions!

Knock, Knock

Who's there?

Snow

Snow who?

Snow business like show business!

DON'T KNOCK IT TIL YOU'VE TRIED IT!

Knock, Knock

Who's there?

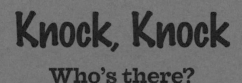

Mary who?

Mary had a little lamb, little lamb, little lamb...*

*Sing this!

Knock, Knock

Who's there?

Baby

Baby who?

Baby shark do do do do do do, baby shark do do do do do do*

*Sing this!

Knock, Knock

Who's there?

Hanna

Hanna who?

Hanna partridge in a pear tree! *

*Sing this!

Knock, Knock

Who's there?

Santa

Santa who?

Wait. Why am I at the door? I'm supposed to come down the chimney!

Knock, Knock

Who's there?

Freeze!

Freeze who?

Freeze a jolly good fellow!
Freeze a jolly good fellow!

KNOCK KNOCK

Knock, Knock

Who's there?

Oswald

Oswald who?

Oswald my chewing gum!

Knock, Knock

Who's there?

Madame

Madame who?

Madame foot's caught in the door!

Knock, Knock

Who's there?

Dinner

Dinnner who?

Dinnner Dinnner
Dinnner Dinnner
Dinnner Dinnner
BATMAN!

Knock, Knock

Who's there?

Beak

Beak who?

Beak careful, the floor is lava!

Knock, Knock

Who's there?

Fur

Fur who?

Fur you, anything!

Knock, Knock

Who's there?

Knot

Knot who?

Knot ready to tell you!

Knock, Knock

Who's there?

Francis

Francis who?

France is where croissants are from.

Knock, Knock

Who's there?

Lass

Lass who?

Round 'em up, cowboy!

Knock, Knock

Who's there?

Sarah

Sarah who?

Sarah McDonalds nearby? I'm starving!

Knock, Knock

Who's there?

Beth

Beth who?

Beth wishes on your birthday!

Knock, Knock

Who's there?

Anita

Anita who?

Anita use the bathroom, hurry up!

DON'T KNOCK IT TIL YOU'VE TRIED IT!

Knock, Knock

Who's there?

I wood wok

I wood wok who?

I wood wok a thousand miles, and I wood wok a thousand more! *

*Sing this!

Knock, Knock

Who's there?

Iris

Iris who?

Iris you a Merry Christmas, Iris you a Merry Christmas, Iris you a Merry Christmas and a Happy New Year!

Knock, Knock

Who's there?

Wanda

Wanda who?

Wanda why it's taking you so long to answer the door?

Knock, Knock

Who's there?

Keith

Keith who?

Keith me, my thweet preenth!

Knock, Knock

Who's there?

Myth

Myth who?

Myth me? (Thorry, I've got a tooth mything)

Knock, Knock

Who's there?

TOEF

Toef who?

THANKS, BUT I'M ALL FULL UP.

Knock, Knock

Who's there?

Gru

Gru who?

You gru five inches since I last saw you.

Knock, Knock

Who's there?

Ivor

Ivor who?

Ivor you let me in, or I'll climb through the window!

DON'T KNOCK IT TIL YOU'VE TRIED IT!

Knock, Knock

Who's there?

Sadie

Sadie who?

Sadie magic word and I'll give you a kiss!

Knock, Knock

Who's there?

She Loves

She Loves Who?

Yeah yeah yeah!

Knock, Knock

Who's there?

Plibbby
McPlubberson

Plibbby McPlubberson who?

Oh come on, how many Plibbby McPlubberson's do you know?

Knock, Knock

Who's there?

You

You who?

You-Hoo?
Anybody home?

Knock, knock!

Who's there?

Stopwatch

Stopwatch who?

Stopwatch you're doing and let me in!

Knock, Knock

Who's there?

Drew

Drew who?

Drew you a bath - because you stink!

Knock, Knock

Who's there?

Pecan

Pecan who?

Pecan somebody your own size!

Knock, Knock

Who's there?

Goose

Goose who?

You tell me - I'm knocking on your door!

DON'T KNOCK IT TIL YOU'VE TRIED IT!

Knock, Knock

Who's there?

Earl

Earl who?

Earl be glad when you go home!

Knock, Knock

Who's there?

WHO LET THE DOGS OUT?

Who let the dogs out who?

WHO! WHO! WHO!

Knock, Knock

Who's there?

Gino

Gino who?

Gino me, now open the door!

Knock Knock!

Who's there?

Yetta

Yetta who?

Yetta nother Knock, Knock joke!

KNOCK IT OFF!

For your reading pleasure, we've scoured the land looking for the very best of the very worst Knock, Knock jokes, and these are the results.

These Knock, Knock jokes are so bad they might just be good. If you want to exact revenge on Mum and Dad for making you tidy your room this morning, tell them a few of these beauts and you'll have them on their knees pleading "KNOCK IT OFF!" in no time.

Knock, Knock

Who's there?

Will

Will who?

Will you marry me?

Knock, Knock

Who's there?

A pile up

A pile up who?

Ewwww!

Knock, Knock

Who's there?

Wood

Wood who?

Wood you like to hear another Knock, Knock joke?

Knock, Knock

Who's there?

VENICE

Venice who?

VENICE IS TIME TO GO HOME?

Knock, Knock

Who's there?

Rough

Rough who?

Rough rough! It's your dog!

Knock, Knock

Who's there?

Bed

Bed who?

Bed you won't like this smell*

*and then fart!

Knock, Knock

Who's there?

RV

RV who?

RV nearly there yet?

Knock, Knock

Who's there?

Shamp

Shamp who?

Not now - but I'll shower later!

Knock, Knock

Who's there?

Oscar

Oscar who?

Oscar silly question, get a silly answer!

Knock, Knock

Who's there?

Russell

Russell who?

Russell up some food, I'm hungry!

Knock, Knock

Who's there?

Riot

Riot who?

Riot on time, here I am!

Knock, Knock

Who's there?

Moose

Moose who?

Moose you be so nosy?

Knock, Knock

Who's there?

Poodle

Poodle who?

Poodle kettle on, please!

Knock, Knock

Who's there?

Iguana

Iguana who?

Iguana hold your hand

Knock, Knock

Who's there?

Goat

Goat who?

Goat to the door and find out!

Knock, Knock

Who's there?

Alpaca

Alpaca who?

Alpaca the trunk, you pack a the suitcase!

Knock, Knock

Who's there?

Scold

Scold who?

Scold outside,
let me in!

Knock, Knock

Who's there?

Dinosaurs

Dinosaurs who?

No, Dinosaurs ROAR!

Knock, Knock

Who's there?

Odysseus

Odysseus who?

Odysseus the last straw!

Knock, Knock

Who's there?

Phil, James, Dan, Paul, Arthur, John, Alex, Rachel, Mark, Annie, Dave, Colin, Ben, Dom, Ellie

Phil, James, Dan, Paul, Arthur, John, Alex, Rachel, Mark, Annie, Dave, Colin, Ben, Dom, Ellie who?

Oh, sorry, wrong door.

Knock, Knock

Who's there?

Nicholas

Nicholas who?

A Nicholas not much money these days.

Knock, Knock

Who's there?

ARTHUR

Arthur who?

ARTHUR GOT!

Knock, Knock

Who's there?

Soup

Soup who?

Souperman

Knock, Knock

Who's There?

Plato

Plato who?

Plato pasta please!

Knock, Knock

Who's there?

Falafel

Falafel who?

Falafel my bike, can you call the doctor!

Knock, Knock

Who's there?

Yoda

Yoda who?

Yoda I am, hmm.

Knock, Knock

Who's there?

Dijiri

Dijiri who?

(Make the sound like a didgeridoo.)

Knock, Knock

Who's there?

Ducks

Duck who?

No, ducks go quack.

Knock, Knock

Who's there?

A mall

A mall who?

A mall shook up!

Knock, Knock

Who's there?

Why!

Why who?

Y-M-C-A!*

*Sing this!

Knock, Knock

Whos there?

Barbara

Barbara who?

Barbara black sheep have you any wool?

Knock, Knock

Whos there?

Rupert

Rupert who?

Rupert your left foot in, your left foot out, in, out, in, out, and shake it all about.*

*Sing this!

Knock Knock

Who's there?

Rhoda!

Rhoda who?

Row, Row, Rhoda boat...*

*Sing this!

Knock, Knock

Who's there?

TOBY

Toby who?

TOBY OR NOT TOBY, THAT IS THE QUESTION.

Knock, Knock

Who's there?

Perth!

Perth who?

Perth-who that robber, he stole my purse!

Knock, Knock

Who's there?

Waiter

Waiter who?

Waiter minute, I just found my keys!

Knock, Knock

Who's there?

Ammonia!

Ammonia who?

Ammonia little girl and I can't reach the doorbell!

Knock, Knock

Who's there?

Dwayne

Dwayne who?

Dwayne the bathtub, I'm dwowning!

Knock, Knock

Who's there?

Boo

Boo who?

Don't cry!

Knock, Knock

Who's there?

Abby

Abby who?

Abby birthday to you!*

*Don't forget to sing this line!

Knock, Knock

Who's there?

Tiss

Tiss who?

A-tiss-who... is for blowing your nose.

Knock, Knock

Who's there?

Tennis

Tennis who?

Tennis five plus five

Knock, Knock

Who's there?

Saul

Saul who?

Saul there is – Bye!